Nelly,

MW00522950

Stay All About
Your Money!

CONSULTANTS

All About My Money

A Guide For
Youth and Young Adults on How to Build,
Manage, and Sustain Wealth

No part of this publication may be reproduced, stored in a retrieval system, or transmitted in any form or by any means — electronic, mechanical, photocopy, recording, or any other — except for brief quotations in printed reviews, without the prior permission of the publisher.

Copyright 2018 © JU Consultants LLC All rights reserved.
ISBN-13: 978-0-692-14413-8
ISBN-10: 0-692-14413-7

Please visit www.juconsultants.com for more information regarding our programs.

Instagram: @juconsultants
Email Address: info@juconsultants.com

ALL ABOUT MY MNEY

A Guide For
Youth and Young Adults on How to Build, Manage, and Sustain Wealth

Jeffrey Ulysse, M.S. Ed.

CONSULTANTS

I dedicate this book in loving memory of my grandfather Estera Ulysse. I only am who I am today because of who you have taught me to be. You are forever missed and always in my thoughts.

And to my mother, father, brother, friends, and mentors. I thank you for your unconditional love and unwavering support.

Contents

Introduction:
Poverty – A Financially
Transmitted Disease

Introduction:
Poverty – A Financially Transmitted Disease

I consider poverty to be an FTD: a Financially Transmitted Disease. In 2016, according to PovertyUSA.org, 21.2% of all children (15.3 million kids) in the United States were living in poverty.1 That's the equivalent of almost 1 in every 5 children. This rapidly spreading ailment of poverty is literally destroying our families and communities, and creating symptoms that lead to financially illiterate and fiscally unstable youth.

Notable symptoms of an FTD infection include mental-health breakdowns, violence, homelessness, and crime. Analyzing state-level data in 2014, the National Center on Family Homelessness found that, nationwide, approximately 2.5 million children experience homelessness each year.[2] These numbers are heartbreaking and gut-wrenching. Millions of children are experiencing this financially transmitted disease!

Our people and our youth are in need of a cure. How can we break this vicious cycle of poverty? What can we do to stop its deadly transmission? Happily, a vaccine already exists: financial literacy and education!

We must spread knowledge of this *vaccine's* existence as if our lives depended upon it—because it *does*. The truth is that young people's lives are in the balance, and—collectively—we must take action. Our young people must learn to combat consumerism, and conquer the beast called *want*. They must learn how to manage their money, build the discipline to save, and discover ways that they can invest and multiply their money by discovering their passions—and learning how to *monetize* the things they love, and love to do.

For far too long, youth culture *makes*, and the world *takes*—and goes ka-ching! With the exception of a handful of high-paid, high-profile celebrities, most young people don't receive due compensation as the originators of the creativity and innovation that keeps not just American mainstream culture, but also global culture, *fresh*. This book aims to help change that.

However, in order to do so, it is important that we radically shift our community consciousness. Sadly for some of us, *broke* has evolved from being circumstantial and a *temporary* condition to a (seemingly) *permanent* lifestyle. Even more concerning is when this mindset goes unchecked, and becomes intergenerational—with unproductivity and lack being handed down like family heirlooms, *from mother to daughter and father to son*.

It is time for us to practice prosperity in our language through affirmative and declarative speaking—and in our actions, through tough choices about fiscal discipline. It is not enough for us to simply admire the rich and covet the objects and toys that they own; it is time for us to leave poor habits behind and embrace the *best* habits of the wealthy.

I know how it feels to experience lack. I once lived from paycheck to paycheck, and was perpetually broke. For far too long I was acquainted with the embarrassment of being forced to borrow from friends and family, and feeling *less than* because I didn't "have." Then I came to the realization that wealth is a mindset, and that I could turn my passion into profit!

This book was deliberately created to generate consciousness, inspire belief, and create action that will manifest itself in abundance and productivity. It is high time for us to divorce broke and marry wealth! As we journey together, know that you can break the back of lack in a single generation—*your* generation! Then hand it off as an enduring legacy to future generations. Change starts with a single decision to do so—change starts now. Let me show you how.

Chapter 1:
Becoming Financially Fit:
Conditioning For Wealth

Chapter 1:
Becoming Financially Fit: Conditioning For Wealth

If you are competing for the Olympics or any competition, fitness is mandatory. There is a level of fitness that is also required when seeking to build, manage, and sustain wealth. In wealth building you can either be financially fit, or you can be a financial misfit. Financial fitness takes discipline, resilience, and relentlessness to accomplish your goals, and to stay on the diet of your budgetary regimen. Becoming a financial misfit is quite easy: You achieve that by becoming a lazy slacker who has no ambition or goals. As such, you have no *why* and that is *why* a life of wealth will pass you by.

We all have the power to get wealthy, but the question is: Are we all *fit* to do so? Healthcare professionals and gyms use a tool to measure an individual's body mass index (or "BMI"). They do this to help to evaluate

We all have the power to get wealthy, but the question is: Are we all fit to do so?

a person's fitness. The BMI is a screening tool that can indicate whether a person is underweight, overweight, or at what is medically accepted as a *healthy* weight. Just like a BMI chart or calculator, you need to have preliminary measures or screening tools in place to identify your level of financial fitness.

Money Mass Index (or "MMI") is the term I've coined to identify and measure your financial fitness for wealth! MMI is measured in the following areas: reading; wealth consciousness; cravings; systems; measurement; talent; and character:

READING

Reading provides intellectual stimulation that is critical to becoming financially fit. Reading has many benefits. Reading keeps your brain active and engaged. It is exercise for the brain that allows it to be healthy, strong, and better able to retain new knowledge. Doctors share that reading could possibly slow the progression, and even prevent, Alzheimer's and dementia in old age.

Reading also expands your vocabulary, and makes you more marketable and valuable. In addition, it improves your focus and concentration, and strengthens your analytical and critical-thinking skills. Reading sets you apart from the competition. It allows you to be a cut above, and ahead of the pack. Simply put: Reading is vital to growth—financial, and in general.

Warren Buffet, whose net worth is over $84 billion dollars, mentioned that one of his keys to success was reading! I've also read that Bill Gates, whose net worth is over $91 billion, reads more than 50 books a year! Their success is living proof that the more you learn, the more you increase your capacity to earn.

WEALTH CONSCIOUSNESS

We define ourselves by what we are conscious of. It is important in the wealth-building process that you first become wealth conscious. There's a saying: *You are what you think*. This means that you are a product of what you are conscious of.

Wealth is a mindset. You have to become conscious of the fact that you *are* wealthy. Before you live it, you must *be* it. You must express it inside of you. You must generate it in your consciousness *first*—before it manifests itself in reality!

> The more you learn, the more you increase your capacity to earn.

Wealth is a mindset that needs to be practiced, developed, and trained. You have to *condition* your mind for wealth. You have to condition your consciousness.

The Wealth Consciousness Formula is designed to create fiscal fitness by generating consciousness. Begin the practice of conditioning your mind for wealth!

Change in mindset + Change in language = Change in behavior

Consistent practice of this formula leads to wealth.

Conversely:

No change in mindset + No change in language = Unchanged behavior
Consistent practice of this formula leads to poverty.

Assess your level of thinking: Do you find that your vocabulary includes words and phrases such as *poor, broke, spend, I don't have,* or *I can't?* Practice positive, affirmative, declarative speaking, and use words like circulate, grow, I will, and the most powerful of all: *I am.* Remember: *Life and death is in the power of the tongue.* You are powerful, and your mouth speaks what you fill your mind with *first!* Then your actions will follow—and bring your thoughts and words to life!

CRAVINGS

Your cravings can either make you or break you. As I mentioned in the previous section: *You are what you think.* Likewise: *You are what you consume.* You become what you are feeding on. If you crave and have an appetite for success, *you become successful.* On the flip side, if you have an appetite for laziness, *you become a sluggard.*

What appetite do you have when it comes to wealth building? Do you feed your needs, or do you feed your wants? What are your priorities when it comes to building wealth? You identify someone's priorities by his or her palate. When speaking about food, a palate relates to your sense of taste, and the *kinds* of things you desire. Similarly, what's your financial palate? Does your appetite lean towards purchasing basic, but solid needs (for the food equivalent, think bread or milk) or luxurious wants (for the food equivalent, think caviar and champagne)? It is important that you have *your* palate under control. It is vital to the wealth-building process that you control your cravings and get into a practice of feeding your needs, not your wants.

Remember: It is imperative that you understand the distinction between needs vs. wants. Ask yourself: Is it really a *need* to purchase a $395 Ferragamo belt, or would it make more sense to invest that $395 into a business-related idea that could help you make more money? Become a disciple of discipline, and remember: *Where there is no order, there is disorder.*

Systems

A system is a formulated plan and/or organized scheme. In order to build wealth, each of these things must be well coordinated.

Wealth building does not come without building a system. You must design a system in order to manage and sustain your wealth. For example, you may decide to set aside a specific percentage of *all* your earnings in a savings account. Personally, I save at least a minimum of ten percent of every check I earn. There will be no sustainability without a system, only mismanagement and instability. Your system needs to be solid, and able to withstand or hold the desired amount of money that you would like to make. Your system has to hold the weight of your aspirations.

What systems do you have in place? This practice will determine if you truly are fit for wealth! If you fail to plan, you plan to fail—and your system will malfunction! Remember: *Poor pockets come from poor planning!*

Measurement

When building wealth, measurement is essential. Measuring helps you know if you are meeting your aims! Without measuring, how will you know if you're on track or off track? It is important to live by measurement. This can be done by creating tools that will allow you to track your progress, such as keeping a journal, planner, and checklist. These practices will help you to determine if you've met your goals.

For example, if you are trying to lose weight, weighing yourself on a scale is critical to identifying if you are on track to meet your goal. Similarly, if you're trying to reach a desired financial state, you have to measure as you build, in order to better manage your money—and to both grow and sustain it over time.

In addition, it is important to attach consequences to the measures or deliverables you establish. Doing so is a way to hold yourself accountable. If you don't meet your *measure* of setting aside ten percent of your money, create a consequence for not meeting that goal. For instance, now you must increase the percentage to be saved on your next earning to fifteen percent as a consequence for not meeting your aim. This practice will keep you consistent, proactive, and productive.

Don't create systems, structures, and goals without designated methods for measuring them! Remember: *What does not get measured does not get met!* The measurements you set in place create sustainability that, like Ford vehicles, is "... tough and built to last!"

TALENT

Cultivate your talent, and grow the gift that's within you: Stop searching outwardly for the gold mine! Have you realized that you *are* the gold mine? Don't just sit around and waste your talents and gifts. Get up and put action behind your passion! For example, if you have a talent for doing hair, nails, and makeup, start marketing to your "clients." Your first clients will likely be those closest to you—your family and friends.

Once you launch your business, document pictures of your most outstanding work, and post them on social media! Doing side-by-side "before" and "after" photos is a particularly great way to show off your skills—and helps to demonstrate to potential

> *Get up and put action behind your passion!*

new clients the kind of work you can do for them, too. If you enjoy baking, bake some cupcakes, document them, and get out there and start funding your dreams!

One more powerful thing you can do to help to market your business is to get "testimonials." If someone raves about your cupcakes, film a video of them "testifying" just how delicious they are, or you can write down your customers' testimonial, and post it online in the form of a "quote" card. Before you post, always make sure that you first get your customer's permission to do so!

CHARACTER

Talent will get you through the door, but character will keep you in the room. Get-rich-quick schemes come at the cost of your future. Wealth earned through diligence and integrity is worth the price! Can you be trusted? Can you be faithful? Can you be consistent? Do you have the type of character that will *keep* you in the room?

ACTIVITY
MMI Self-Assessment
Screening

ACTIVITY
MMI Self-Assessment Screening

READING

As I previously mentioned, Bill Gates—one of the wealthiest men in the world, with an estimated net worth of $91 billion, and climbing—says he reads over 50 books a year. This is an example of how we should glean from the best practices of the rich! Bill Gates says that reading gives him a competitive edge, and tests his understanding. As the saying goes: Reading is fundamental. True, indeed. Reading is a fundamental and foundational tool in building, managing, and sustaining wealth!

Let's do a financial-fitness exercise, and take an introspective plunge and see where we are: Ready, set, dive!...

How many books do you read per month? _____

How many books have you read within the past six months? _____

How many books have you read this past year?

_____

OK, make your way back up and take a breath.

Now, let's set some goals and sharpen each other!

How many books will you commit to reading per month?

_____

How many books will you commit to reading this year?

_____

 *FIT TIP – THE MORE YOU LEARN, THE MORE YOU EARN*

WEALTH CONSCIOUSNESS – YOUR RELATIONSHIP WITH MONEY

Have you ever considered how you keep your money? Take some time and analyze how you treat your money. For example, do you treat your money like it's your friend—with love, care, and respect? Or do you mistreat your money, and crumple your bills and stuff them in your wallet, and have a tendency to lose money? How do you treat your money? Be honest:

_____

_____

_____

_____

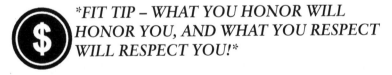

FIT TIP – WHAT YOU HONOR WILL HONOR YOU, AND WHAT YOU RESPECT WILL RESPECT YOU!

Are you "wealth" conscious or "lack" conscious? Do you find, in the way you think and use your words, that you have a tendency to emphasize and glorify your lack, rather than your wealth?

_____

_____

_____

_____

 *FIT TIP – WEALTH IS A MINDSET*

CONQUERING CRAVINGS – LET'S DO A TASTE TEST!

Ask yourself: *What kind of taste do I have? Am I simple and modest, or do I have expensive taste?* Be honest:

_____

_____

_____

_____

_____

_____

Living within your means doesn't mean that you have to quit dreaming big! Just because you can't have it now doesn't mean that you aren't going to get it one day. Not spending beyond your means is actually not a bad thing. The rich are quite frugal with their money! (#facts) You must be disciplined, and able to conquer desire, if you're serious about become rich yourself!

Systems and structures – Tools for money management

Real talk, ask yourself:

When money comes into my hand what do I *FIRST* think about doing with it?

_____

_____

_____

_____

When money comes into my hand what do I actually do with it?

_____

_____

_____

Have you ever thought about creating a system around what to do with your money when it actually arrives? What are three systems and structures you can create for your money?

_____

_____

_____

_____

FIT TIP – A LIFE WITHOUT SYSTEMS IS A LIFE WITHOUT ORDER, AND A LIFE WITHOUT ORDER IS LIKE LIVING WITH HOLES IN YOUR POCKETS AND WALLET!

MEASUREMENT – WHAT DOES NOT GET MEASURED DOES NOT GET MET!

What measurements do I have in place NOW, so I will know that I am meeting my goal?

_____

_____

_____

_____

What measures CAN I put in place that will allow me to see if I'm meeting my goals and targets?

_____

_____

_____

_____

Talent – Mine your hidden treasures

What are your talents—things that you do effortlessly well and people compliment you on? What are your passions—things that bring you a sense of fulfillment by your doing and solving them? (NOTE: Once you discover what these things are, you can turn them into a "niche" business that pays you!

_____

_____

_____

_____

*FIT TIP – IT'S TIME FOR YOU TO PUT SOME ACTION BEHIND YOUR PASSION!

Chapter 2:
Money Management –
Poor Pockets Come from
Poor Planning

Chapter 2:
Money Management – Poor Pockets Come from Poor Planning

You will never be able to build, manage, or sustain wealth if you do not understand how to manage your money. Money management is a plan you design to control your money. The true nature of money management is really wrapped in one word: *budgeting.*

A budget is a financial plan that you use to manage your money, which also allows you to save and grow your money over time. The only way wealth can be sustainable is if it is managed properly, and according to a budget.

It is important to understand that if you do not create a budget plan, you are *planning* to go broke. There is no growth without proper money management. When you fail to plan or manage your money, you are just saying to the universe that *you are not fit for wealth.*

Poor pockets come from poor planning. Conversely: Proper planning prevents poor pockets. So what am I saying? Proper budgeting creates healthy habits that lead to building wealth. On the other hand, the inability to budget results in poor habits that lead to lack.

However, it is not enough to *plan* your budget—you have to *work* your budget! When you begin to work your budget plan, your budget plan becomes your employee, and works for you!

Poor pockets come from poor planning. Conversely: Proper planning prevents poor pockets.

We have to become more frugal and combat consumerism by making a commitment to budgeting. We live in a society that glorifies the luxurious lifestyle, but it's important that we learn and understand where we *realistically* are financially, and develop the discipline to embrace living according to our means.

That is not to say that we will never be able to reach the place where we can enjoy some of life's finer things. However, managing your money is about building and creating a plan that will allow you to get to that desired place, and level up.

Wealth is not something that occurs or happens overnight. Wealthy individuals who sustain wealth master the art of budgeting. Wealthy individuals understand what it means to be faithful and consistent with the *little things*. If you're faithful with the *little* things, you'll be ready for the *big things*. Money management is all about demonstrating faithfulness, discipline, and consistency in the small decisions that you make concerning your money.

Budgeting is essential to becoming fit for wealth. If you are tired of seeing your money dissipate, and if you're tired of living like you've got holes in your pockets, then it's time that you start budgeting!

One great tip for helping you to manage your money is creating a budget diary. Before you can effectively manage your spending, you have to see where your money is going on a daily basis. You have to track your money, and creating a budget diary is like placing a tracer on your cash. You are able to see your income and expenses, and you're also able to identify if you have a budget surplus, with money left over, or a budget deficit, where you have less cash that you *thought* you had.

Here is an example of a sample budget diary that you can incorporate into your daily life:

Date	Description	Category	Amount
5|30|18	"All About My Money" Book	Expense/ Need	$25.00

ACTIVITY
Money Management – Creating a Simple Budget

ACTIVITY
Money Management – Creating a Simple Budget

Let's do a quick and simple exercise

Scenario 1: Part A

Maria gets $15 a week for her allowance. In addition, she recently celebrated her birthday and received $450 in cash from her family. Also, this past month, Maria babysat her neighbor's daughter and was paid $100.

1. What was Maria's total income for the month?

_____

Maria wants to hang out with her friends on Saturday in Downtown Brooklyn. She plans to go shopping at American Eagle to buy a sweater for $54.95 and a pair of jeans for $49.95. Afterward, she wants to eat out at Applebee's and get the two-for-$20 meal. At the end of that evening they want to catch a movie at the theater on Court Street, which will cost her $15.50. Maria also needs a round-trip Metro card that will cost her $5.50.

2. Identify Maria's expenses—for now, only the items, not their cost:

_____

_____

_____

_____

3. Place a dollar amount against each of her expenses:

_____

_____

_____

_____

4. What is Maria's budget surplus, if applicable?

_____

_____

_____

_____

Scenario 1: Part B Place your calculations into the budget template below

Income	Expenses	Budget Surplus
Allowance:	Food:	How much money has been left over? Please list the dollar amount below.
Gifts/Donations:	Clothing:	
Chores/Part-time Job:	Transportation:	
Other:	Entertainment:	
Income total:_____	Expenses total: _____	Surplus total: _____

Ask yourself: *What steps can I take to better manage my money?*

_____

_____

_____

_____

 FIT TIP: IF YOU DON'T PLAN ON MANAGING YOUR MONEY, YOU'RE PLANNING TO GO BROKE!

Chapter 3:
Saving – Where There Is No Vision, There Can Be No Provision

Chapter 3:
Saving – Where There Is No Vision, There Can Be No Provision

Saving is all about preservation. It's about being thrifty and, quite honestly, economical. When we talk about the topic of saving, we're really asking how can we be more economical and frugal with our money?

Saving is something that is not an easy task. In fact, it can feel like a sacrificial task. However, saving has many benefits when implemented. First off, savings serves as your safety net.

When you're running low on funds, you have something to dip into. When life gives you lemons, you can make lemonade, because you've got something that was sitting in a bank account, piggy bank, pillow, or shoebox.

Saving is the ultimate test of self-discipline. You have to have the discipline to say: *No, I don't need that right now OR I won't buy this item that I don't need, just because it's on sale.* You have to have self-discipline if you're going to conquer the beast called want.

You've got to make a decision when it comes to saving: *Will I meet my needs, or will I feed my wants?* In order to do so, you have to understand the difference between a need and want. It is important that when it comes to saving, you have to *conquer* wants. Want is a parasite that "needs" to suck you dry, in order for it to live. Want sucks the life out of your ability to save. Want is very selfish. However, need is selfless. Focusing on your needs and saving your money is critical to the wealth-building process.

I would like to open your understanding and give you another perspective on savings. Saving is all about your ability to see. You can only *have* as far as you can *see*. What am I saying? *I am saying that as far as you can see is as far as you can save!* Saving is all about having a vision. You cannot save without a vision. If you have no vision, you won't make *provision for the vision.*

> It's never too early, and you're never too young to start saving your money!

So the question is: *What do you see?* Where do you see yourself in the next five years? Where do you see yourself in the next ten years? How far you can see determines how much you can save.

The writer, Ralph Waldo Emerson, said that you can live the life that you have imagined. However, you can only live the life that you've imagined if you can see that life. Can you see that life that you've imagined for yourself? If so, start saving for that life now! Remember: It's never too early, and you're never too young to start saving your money!

ACTIVITY
Saving

ACTIVITY
Saving

Let's explore saving through the following financial-fitness exercises:

1. What is the importance of saving, and why should you care?

_____

_____

_____

_____

2. What prevents you from saving money?

_____

_____

_____

_____

3. Ask yourself: *What can I do better to save my money?*

_____

_____

_____

_____

The famous self-help author, Napoleon Hill, said, "You can be anything you want to be, if only you believe with sufficient conviction and act in accordance with your faith; for whatever the mind can conceive and believe, the mind can achieve." Well, you might ask what in the world does this have to do with saving?

Here's what: In order to save, you have to save with a sense of purpose and intentionality. Aimless saving leads to loss—as in, you don't have a target, and will quickly spend what you've saved. In other words, you spend money when you have no vision. You save money when you have an ultimate goal that keeps you on track! Purposeful saving leads to profit. Successful saving only happens when you can SEE IT—whatever it is for you!

In this exercise we are going to do together: We are going to SEE and REEL in your short-term and long-term goals.

1. Think it.

Take a moment to ponder:

Where do you see yourself in the next five years?

Where do you see yourself in the next ten years?

_____

_____

_____

_____

2.Believe it.

What are some practical steps you can take towards strengthening your belief in your vision?

_____

_____

_____

_____

*FIT TIP – REMEMBER, WHATEVER YOUR MIND CAN CONCIEVE AND BELIEVE, YOU CAN ACHIEVE! GET INTO THE PRACTICE OF FEEDING YOUR BELIEFS AND STARVING YOUR DOUBTS.

3.See it!

Let's take a moment and do a mindfulness "time-travel" activity. I want you to relax, close your eyes, inhale, exhale, and visualize where you will be in the next five years.
OK, open your eyes.
Now visualize where you see yourself in the next ten years.

You did it: You have *traveled to the future!*

FIT TIP – YOU CAN HAVE AS FAR AS YOU CAN SEE. REMEMBER: SEE IT AND REEL IT IN!

4. Write it down!

You're almost done: Now write down the vision and make it clear! Summarize in one to two sentences where you see yourself in the next five years.

_____

_____

_____

_____

Summarize in one to two sentences where you see yourself in the next ten years.

_____

_____

_____

_____

After time traveling, you were able to "see" yourself five and ten years from now.

Based off of your five-year vision, what are some things you can begin to save for _now_, to position you to reel in your future?

_____

_____

_____

_____

You saw yourself ten years from now! What are some things you can begin to save for *now* to position you to reel in your future?

_____

_____

_____

_____

5. Speak it!

The law of attraction says: *What you speak, you will attract.* Your words are powerful and magnetic! Let's do something really cool, and confuse gravity for a second and tell the universe three times out loud where you're going to be in the next five years and ten years! Ready, set, go! one, two, three—now shout it out! Awesome.

List five tangible and practical things that you can do *now* to prepare yourself for your destiny. Your destiny is not a matter of luck: It's an intentional decision!

1. _____

2. _____

3. _____

4. _____

5. _____

Chapter 4:
Investing – The Money-Making Machine

Chapter 4:
Investing – The Money-Making Machine

The mind is your money-making machine. I believe that currency is not the physical money that you see. I believe it is a product of the ideas that come from the mind—your money-making machine. Your ideas are Golden Seeds called currency that when they are cultivated, planted, and watered create a money tree.

Have you ever seen a fruit called a pomegranate? A pomegranate, has many seeds—and so does your mind. The mind is like a pomegranate, but with Golden Seeds called ideas that when planted and tended to create the money tree I spoke about!

Now think about it: Where does the next big project or the next big thing or idea come from? They come from your ideas, which come from your mind: your money-making machine! You have been designed with one of the greatest gifts of all: *the mind!*

Your ideas create currency. Think about how many ideas and thoughts that we have per day. Now think about how much money you're probably sitting on or passing up, because you have not taken that passing idea captive.

What idea have you had burning in you? What is that idea that you have that you can invest in, cultivate, and turn into a product that *pays* you?

> You have been designed with one of the great-est gifts of all: the mind!

It's time to apply action to your passion. It's time to grab a shovel and start digging. It's time for you to live the life that you've imagined. Wealth is attainable, and the Golden Seeds of prosperity are in all of us, regardless of race, gender, or class.

What next "big" thing or idea do you have sitting inside of you? Take it captive, write it down, and work toward making it happen!

- _____
- _____
- _____
- _____
- _____

FIT TIP: GOLDEN SEEDS OF PROSPERITY ARE IN ALL OF US!

Chapter 5:
Passion to Profit - From Chasing The Bag To The Bag Chasing You

Chapter 5:
Passion to Profit - From Chasing The Bag To The Bag Chasing You

In youth culture today, we talk about "chasing paper," or "chasing the bag." Although these phrases maybe trendy, cool, or in season, that is poor thinking. I believe that we have to radically shift consciousness and change our perception. We must generate a sense of consciousness that transitions from chasing the bag to the bag chasing *you*!

How can you go from working for your money to your money working for you? The phrase chasing the bag is equivalent to you working for your money. Companies like Supreme have generated the consciousness of the bag chasing them, and all you see are lines wrapped around blocks. They turned their passion into a product that created market value and profit.

> **We must generate a sense of consciousness that transitions from chasing the bag to the bag chasing you!**

Oftentimes, we find ourselves perfectly willing to take the risk of investing our money in stocks or other income sources, meanwhile neglecting to invest in the greatest reward of all: our *passions*. Could you possibly be sitting on a gold-mine idea—and what you are seeking to invest in externally already exists internally: *in your mind?*

You can turn your passion into profit, and make it liquid. You can also take what you are passionate about and generate solutions to the challenges and breakdowns that our society is currently facing.

In order for you to turn your passion into profit, you first need to identify what your passion is. In addition, if you find that you have multiple passions and do them well, I encourage you to see them as multiple streams of income. However, if you have multiple passions and do multiple things well, it is *very important* to master one, and then master the next one after that. Make a decision today and invest in yourself!

Now let's get ready to do a financial-fitness exercise to identify your passion!

ACTIVITY
Identifying Your Passion

ACTIVITY
Identifying Your Passion

Ask yourself:

1. What do I have a genuine love for?

_____

_____

_____

_____

2. What is it that I love so much that I would even do it for free?

_____

_____

_____

_____

3. What is it that moves me, drives me, and gives me a natural high?

_____

_____

_____

_____

4. What is it that I do effortlessly and naturally well, where it's like I've got the "Midas touch"—and everything I do related to that gifting turns to *gold*?

_____

_____

_____

_____

_____

_____

_____

_____

5. If you find that you have multiple passions where you've got the Midas touch, list them all below, as potential multiple income streams! Remember, master one then master the others—one at a time!

A. _____

B. _____

C. _____

D. _____

E. _____

 FIT TIP: PUT SOME ACTION BEHIND YOUR PASSION!

Chapter 6:
Habitudes Part 1: The Habits of the Wealthy, Rich and Famous

Chapter 6:
Habitudes Part 1: The Habits of the Wealthy, Rich and Famous

Masters of Time

There are 24 hours in a day. The rich understand how to make the most of the day and redeem the time! They demonstrate mastery over their day by scheduling, creating to-do lists, and displaying efficient time management.

Planners and Doers

Proper planning prevents both poor performance and poor pockets. However, the wealthy see that it is not sufficient just to plan their work, but also *to work their plan*. As they work their plan, their plan becomes their employee!

GOAL Getters

The wealthy, and rich and famous are goal getters who live by measures. They set goals, and get those goals done! How can you meet an aim that is not set, and how can you know that you have met your aim without measuring it? What does not get measured simply will not, and cannot, be met. Period.

EXERCISE AND MEDITATION

Mindfulness meditation and physical exercise impact the brain and physical body positively. Mindfulness meditation is having the ability to be fully aware, awake and present *in the moment*. Both create a heightened sense of mental aptitude and awareness that leads to less fatigue and increased performance. It is important to bring your mind in balance, and to subject your body to the physical discipline of exercise.

RAVENOUS READERS

The more you learn, the more you earn! Feeding your mind is just as important as feeding your body. As previously mentioned, reading creates new knowledge pathways, and is vital to the procreation of innovation!

EARLY RISERS

The early bird gets the worm! You have to want success more than you want to snooze a couple more minutes or sleep several more hours! Ever heard the phrase: *You snooze you lose?* One word: Truth.

Problem Solvers

The wealthy live in a world called solutions. They see the difficult issues in the world, but focus on generating answers to such breakdowns. Living in the world called solutions causes you to be a money magnet.

Networkers

The rich and famous cultivate relationships and grow their network! They understand that their network determines their net worth! They surround themselves and rub shoulders with those who are more astute, wiser, and wealthier than they are. If you rub shoulders with those who are wealthy, you begin to absorb the practices and mindset you need to become wealthy yourself. Conversely, if you surround yourself with poor, toxic relationships, guess what?.... You got it.

Frugal Spenders

The rich are quite frugal. They save and live on a budget! When it comes to shopping, they are serious bargainers, hunting for a good deal—more often than not—rather than paying full price.

GIVERS

Time is money. Volunteering your time and giving your money increases your capacity to receive more. Money is currency. Currency is all about movement and flow. When you give, you cause a current of currency to flow that will end up flowing right back to you in good measure!

Chapter 7:
Habitudes Part. 2: The Habits of the Broke, Busted, and Disgusted

Chapter 7: Habitudes Part. 2: The Habits of the Broke, Busted, and Disgusted

MASTERS OF PROCRASTINATION

We mentioned that the rich are masters of time. However, the broke are masters of procrastination. They fail to seize the day, and rather than create to-do lists and schedules, they create excuses. Those with a poverty mindset are subject, and fall prisoner, to the demands of the day, while the rich control time throughout their day.

POOR PLANNERS AND DOERS

Know this: By failing to prepare, you are preparing to fail. The broke live with holes in their pockets and wallets, based on their failure to effectively plan, prepare, and execute.

GOAL-LESS

The broke are goal-less, and have no target to meet their aims. Again: Without a vision, how can there ever be provision? Talk is cheap.

MENTALLY UNFIT

Those who are mentally unfit fail to create time for meditation and exercise. They often find themselves frustrated, stressed, and perplexed. If you are mentally and physically unstable, how can you truly be fit for wealth? If you are always sick, how can you enjoy your wealth? Remember, your mental health is also a form of wealth.

DISPASSIONATE READERS

Mark Twain once said, "The man who does not read, has no advantage over the man who cannot read." In other words: If you're able to read, but don't *exercise* your power to read, then you might as well be illiterate. Those who wish to remain poor have no desire or appetite for reading, which leaves them complacent about their circumstances, incompetent, and incapable of growing in knowledge and understanding. They remain mental dwarfs, with no capacity for growth or innovation.

SNOOZERS AND LOSERS

The broke, busted, and disgusted prefer to snooze and lose, rather than wake up early, ready to move and cruise towards the finish line for their goals!

PROBLEM ORIENTED

The broke are problem oriented. They are so fixated on issues, they begin to feel helpless and hopeless. They do not realize that they can change their situation or circumstance by focusing on the things that they *can control*, and creating a change in their mindset.

NETWORK ERROR

Those with a poverty mindset fail to cultivate relationships and grow their network. If you rub shoulders with those that are broke, busted, and disgusted, who and what do you expect to become?

CARELESS SPENDERS

The broke are careless and wasteful with their spending. They live beyond their means and mismanage their money. The last thing they consider is saving money, because the first thing they consider is feeding their wants. I encourage every young person and young adult to evaluate your spending habits, and begin the practice of saving. Whether it's five or ten percent—or more—it all adds up! Take advantage of your youth, when you don't yet have heavy expenses and responsibilities, such as a mortgage, or student-loan repayments. Don't be a *careless* spender; be a careful one.

HOARDERS

Those who choose to be stingy and tight fisted with their money fail to realize that in doing so, they are blocking the current of currency from flowing their way. The universal law of reciprocity recognizes those who give by giving them even more!

ACTIVITY
Time to Reflect

ACTIVITY
Time to Reflect

After reviewing the habits of the rich and those with a poverty mindset, let's do a financial-fitness self-check!

1. What strategies can you implement to help you become a "master of time," and improve your time management, to make the most of your 24 hours each day?

_____

_____

_____

_____

2. How much money would you like to generate?

_____

_____

_____

3. After listing your desired amount of money, what is the "plan" and next steps can you take to reach that figure?

_____

_____

_____

_____

_____

_____

_____

_____

4. Do you make any time for exercise and meditation? If not, can you identify any barriers or stumbling blocks that are in your way that have kept you from doing so?

_____

_____

_____

_____

_____

_____

_____

5. Are you a ravenous reader, or a disinterested reader? How can you grow your passion for, and relationship with reading?

_____

_____

_____

_____

_____

_____

1. What dangers are there in oversleeping or making a habit of hitting the snooze button? In this exercise, go the extra mile and come up with some dangers specific to *you.*

_____

_____

_____

_____

_____

_____

2. Do you find that you tend to focus more on problems than the solutions? If so, why? What can you do to change that?

_____

_____

_____

_____

_____

_____

_____

3. Name at least five mentors or people in your life who motivate, challenge, and encourage you to reach higher.

_____

_____

_____

_____

_____

_____

_____

4. Are you careless or careful with your money? Do you consider saving money at all? If so, how much do you consider saving? If not, why don't you consider saving money?

_____

_____

_____

_____

_____

_____

5. Do you like to volunteer and donate, or do you find it hard to let go of your time and money?

_____

_____

_____

_____

_____

_____

6. What habits do you feel you need to improve, and why?

_____

_____

_____

_____

_____

_____

_____

 FIT TIP: THERE IS POWER IN THE PROCESS, TRUST IT

Chapter 8:
Credit – Live Up to Your Name

Chapter 8:
Credit – Live Up to Your Name

I have always thought about credit as your name. Your credit is your name, which is the key to your identity, brand, money, and fame. One of the things that I have come to understand is that a good name is better than gold or silver!

When it comes to your name, you have to protect it by all means. As your name relates to your credit—as in your actual credit score, and ability to get credit from other individuals, or an institution like a bank—you have to protect and preserve your name at all costs.

First, it's important to understand credit and the way that it works. Credit is very important to the wealth-building process, because credit can create debt. Bear in mind that debt could be bad *or* good, and that debt being "positive" or "negative" depends on a variety of factors, many of which are specific to *you*, and your individual situation.

I remember my first day in college, at our orientation session, all of the credit card companies were lined up at a table, trying to get all of us new students to sign up for credit cards. They tried to entice us by talking about all the great offers and benefits. I remember I and all my friends thinking that if we signed up, were signing up for a FREE $1,000—just like that!

Not so fast....

I wonder how many students are presented with this opportunity, and fall prey to signing up for something that they are not yet a good fit for. The offer sounds great, but what a lot of young people who haven't had credit before don't know is that there is a limit to your credit line, and if you exceed that, you can max your card out—and be hit with costly penalties and fees.

What many of them don't know about are the monthly payments that will follow that credit card purchase. Many also don't know how only making the minimum monthly payment on an item—instead of paying it all off when the first bill comes—can keep them financially enslaved for years in order to pay off a big-ticket item!

In the meantime, the interest charges and fees keep piling up. What many of them fail to realize is that what you borrow, you have to pay back *on time*. Many who lack this knowledge up front end up falling behind on payments, losing their cards, and "messing" up their credit—which can make it difficult to get credit later not for *wants*, but for *needs* like getting a student loan, or a loan to open up a business.

When you fail to pay back what you borrowed, your credit—that is, your "name"—takes a hit, and it affects your ability to build and prepare for your future.

What many young people inexperienced with credit don't know is that how we use our credit is being measured by a credit score, which lenders, like banks and other institutions, review to see if and how *well you have lived up to your name.* Before they choose to invest or lend to you, these institutions want to see if you "Walk It" like you "Talk It."

It is very important to understand the role of credit in the wealth-building process. *Debt is the enemy of wealth, and the friend of poverty.* It is critical that you avoid *unnecessary* debt at all costs. Again, not all debt is bad—but debt should be a last resort, even for good reasons, like paying for college or opening a business.

First see if there are other ways to finance if not all, then most, of such costs through other means—for instance, researching and applying for college scholarships. Where there's too much debt, there can be no

> Debt is the enemy of wealth, and the friend of poverty

sustainability. You say you're trying to get wealthy, but you'll notice that you're not succeeding, because you're too busy paying off all the debt you accumulated, while simultaneously proving by your lack of financial fitness, because *you couldn't live up to your name*. Live up to your name—and not down, by crushing your name under a truckload of debt!

Before applying for a credit card ask yourself the following questions:

1. Do I really understand what credit is all about?

2. Am I prepared to live up to the responsibility of having a credit card?

3. Do I really need a credit card right now?

4. Can I be faithful and trusted to pay back what I borrowed in a timely manner?

Chapter 9: The Final Transaction – Paid in Full

Chapter 9: The Final Transaction – Paid in Full

In order for us to become fit for wealth, we must first accomplish the foundational principle of generating consciousness. You can come into millions of dollars and lose it just like that because you have not generated the consciousness and the level of fitness in character that produces sustainability. How many times have you seen lottery winners of millions or tens of millions of dollars who start off broke before their win—and end up broke again?

I heard a phrase that says: "How do you eat an elephant? One bite at a time!" It is the same with building, managing, and sustaining wealth: You have to take it piece-by-piece, and step-by-step.

We must share the message and vaccination of financial empowerment in our communities. It is vital that our youth and young adults grow up to become owners and not renters, lenders and not borrowers.

I encourage you to begin to practice budgeting and saving now!

I encourage you to invest in the greatest stock of all: *yourself!* Try to maintain full ownership over your ideas, and any business you create. However, if a seemingly great opportunity comes along to *cash in* on your idea (by selling your business, or simply taking on an additional investor), remember your worth, and never sell your stock *cheap*—know your value!

I encourage and implore you that every single morning when you wake up looking in the mirror, declare to yourself that your broke days are over, and that your wealthy days have begun!

I encourage you to grab a shovel, start digging, and put some action behind your passion! Likewise: Translate your foggy passions into liquid funds—by creating a plan on how to do so.

I encourage you to see your mind as a money-making machine, and capture every brilliant, creative thought you have, turn them over and examine them, and see if you can turn them into...Golden Seeds!

I encourage you to see that wealth is not just for a certain class or race, but it is for those who choose to generate it in their consciousness and take action.

Use the insights and principles I've shared with you to stay all about *your* money, in a way that lets you build, manage, and sustain wealth—for the *rest* of your life!

BONUS CHAPTER

BONUS CHAPTER

"My Wishes For A Young Generation"

I wish you more life and more time to reach more heights.

We keep telling you to reach for the stars,

but fail to help you fly.

Well, I wish you more flight.

I wish you more nights up, restless, can't sleep because you can't stop thinking about your goals—I hope you reach them.

I wish you'd see where society keeps trying to trip you up, sets traps so you could fail—I wish it'd make you more "tight."

I wish you'd stay mad and stay vocal, say I won't accept anything beneath the best for yourself; I wish you'd stay fired up; I wish you don't give up; I wish you more fight.

I wish you'd learn from your mistakes, do less wrong, and do more right.

I wish you'd stay in the sun, continuing to glow through the dark spaces.

May many men remember your faces. You shine already, but I wish you more light.

I wish you'd take a quick break from social media to stop searching for more likes, and receive more love.

I wish you food on the table; all your bills paid; money in the bank; a job you truly desire; a 401(k); vacations fully paid; everything taken care of, because you take care of yourself.

I wish your hair and nails stay done ladies; haircuts forever fresh fellas; I wish you always look your best, so you never miss an opportunity.

I wish you'd look at all the beautiful people around you and start with yourself

I wish you prosperity, I wish you good health.

I wish you'd see school as a tool to advance you; I wish you'd use it as a token;

I wish you'd think of higher education; I wish it'd make you more hype.

For your future, I wish you happiness:

That life would get more nice; that work would feel more like passion and not punishment for a paycheck; that everyone who says they ever loved you would treat you with respect; that you expect nothing but the best; that

you have open eyes to see the world not just from your nest, but that you get more sight. That you get a taste of success, then get more bites.

I wish you never stop learning how to be the best version of yourself; that you learn not just how to make money, but that you learn how to create wealth—that you live WELL and never see a CELL.

That your mind can flourish in freedom and never become like jail.

That you find the love of your life, and y'all gel—come together and build an empire and propel HIGHER.

I wish you well, and if you fail, you still see value in yourself and get back up again, because the future's more bright.

I wish your mistakes would make you wiser, so that you grow no matter what.

Above all, you live to WIN even when you lose, and you earn more stripes.

I wish in the media you see more types of success stories from people who look just like you, so you can identify and be inspired, and your inspiration can go inspire another person more like you—and the cycle continues.

I say a prayer for you;
I make it clear for you;

I'm here for you all because I care for you all;
I stare at you all;
And I see beasts in you all;
I got faith in you all;
Don't let me down.

Latoya "Tee Lectual" Semple Forrester
Spoken Word Artist
Instagram Handle: @tee_lectual

About the Author

Jeffrey Ulysse is a Brooklyn born award-winning youth leader, motivational speaker, author, youth leader, and founder and CEO of JU Consultants. JU Consultants is a youth-development and educational consulting company that has been featured on Brooklyn News 12, and offers services such as youth financial education; young men's and girls' empowerment programs; "artivism"; "edutainment" pep rallies and seminars; professional development; public speaking; and coaching.

This year in 2018, JU Consultants partnered with Capital One Bank and the Brooklyn Borough President's office on a Brooklyn wide Youth Financial Education Tour, empowering over 1,500 young people in over fifteen schools and communities in nine Brooklyn community districts in neighborhoods such as Bedford Stuyvesant and Brownsville.

Jeffrey has both a Bachelor's degree in health science and a Master's of Science in Education, both from Long Island University. In addition, he is receiving his second Master's degree, in divinity, from Virginia Union University, and plans to pursue a doctoral degree in youth development and family studies.

Jeffrey is a visionary who is compelled by his love for young people. He receives his greatest joy and fulfillment from seeing young people fully awakened to their potential and purpose. He desires nothing more than to share in the triumphs of those who were once idle, purposeless, and held captive by low expectations and low self-esteem. Jeffrey believes his purpose in life is to revolutionize youth development, radically influence our times, and pave the way for a generation to dream and create the lives they have imagined.

For inquiries and bookings:

info@juconsultants.com
www.juconsultants.com
Instagram Handle: @juconsultants

REFERENCES

1. Poverty Facts: The Population of Poverty USA: http://www.povertyusa.org/facts

2. Ibid.